THE NEXT INFINITY

Also by Nancy Botkin

Parts That Once Were Whole

Bent Elbow and Distance

In Waves

Signs of Life

THE
NEXT
INFINITY

∞

POEMS BY

NANCY BOTKIN

Broadstone

Library of Congress Control Number 2019941688

ISBN 978-1-937968-60-1

Text & Cover Design by Larry W. Moore

Cover artwork by the author,
used by permission

Broadstone Books
An Imprint of
Broadstone Media LLC
418 Ann Street
Frankfort, KY 40601-1929
BroadstoneBooks.com

Contents

FOUR

ONE

Skin

I heard the word *skin*.
The song's chorus pounded *skin
the bottle*, but, alas, it was *spin*.
I like skin better.
That a bottle could have it,
and it could be pulled away
from its curves, more
sensuous than violent, like
peeling an orange.
I once typed *lies* rather than *lives*,
skipping over the *v*.
She lies in South Bend.
I lie there too, once in a hammock
while I lied through my teeth
with my silence, or was it
with those little o's a fish makes?
My upper lip moist, my hand
slipping from the glass, the sun
my curse, my sweet enemy,
July petals quivering,
making softness, making red.

RIGHT ANGELS

They mean angles,
        of course, my students
who rely on spell checker.
        Who are the right angels,
and are there left angels?
        The nuns told us we all had
a guardian angel
        which, in my mind,
didn't protect my neighbor Fritz,
        afflicted with cerebral palsy,
his feet scraping
        along the driveway,
one crutch banging
        my dad's new car.
Nor did it protect
        the young couple's
daughter, the bicycle accident,
        the brain hemorrhage.
There are layers and layers
        in misspellings,
and perhaps my dad's angel
        went dark the day
his bare foot landed
        on a bee, or when,
pencil behind his ear,
        he hit his thumb with
a hammer trying to square up
        the angles, cursing
the Lord and the Lord's
        mother and father,
and every holy saint
        he could think of while
I crossed myself (up
        down left right) before
exploding into the unknown
        world with its intricate patterns
and ghostly shadows,
        its angling wings.

Same Rain, Same City

1.

I'd go back and start again
if I could walk the trail along the gold coast,

catch the rising star,
enter without rest my immaculate story.

But chances are I'd end up standing in the same rain,
in the same city where the history of light

is open to interpretation. Light
in which everything can be reckoned or not.

In the glow of dusk a girl runs to meet a boy near
the railroad tracks, and as the low whistle sounds,

the deer come out to graze at the edge of the woods.
It begins to snow lightly, a flake or two settling

on her wool coat, enough to astonish him, enough
to make him think he'll be there whenever beauty turns up.

2.

After snow and rain, skies that have whitened
or gone blood-red over calm bodies of water,

I arrive at the place where my father stands
in front of the mirror touching his tired,

slack face which appears flawless
when he looks at me for the last time.

Not me next to him, but the reflected me.
We're both speeding alongside the ticking

silver river, but whose name shall we use?
Who will stand up to claim us?

Cityscapes ablaze with neon, mirrors within mirrors,
are enough to make me want to begin again.

WE'RE OKAY IN THE HEARTLAND

We're okay in the heartland.
Some dolls are missing their arms,

but that's to be expected.
We arrange our still lifes on the heavy

linen our grandmothers saved
from the old country. We're obsessed

with birds, although we fumble their names.
Pleasure comes when they leave in a rush,

or balance together on a thin black wire.
We convince ourselves that all we need

to live on is one fragile ghost and the roaring
circus in our own backyard. We gravitate

toward a warmer palette, damp ground,
difficult light. Our sleep aided by a

whistling train in one ear, and the infinite
echoes of ocean tides in the other.

LOVE IS BLUE

I find myself gulping for air which has no melody.
　　　　At best, it's cymbals crashing. Blue ocean
as far as I can see, and my body in love with water. My body
　　　　in love with undercurrents. These are difficult
matters. During revolutions people destroy their own artifacts,
　　　　create a million cacophonies. All that fire. All that roaring.
You'd think lighting a match would be clean and simple.
　　　　Long ago in high school a girl crumpled her math test
before bending over a small mirror to apply mascara
　　　　in a sweeping motion while the rest of us were solving for x.
The enraged teacher stood next to her desk. She paused and held
　　　　the raised wand like an orchestra conductor. Without taking her eyes
off the teacher, she brought it down slowly so that everyone
　　　　in the room would continue believing in music.

POLL

In what do you believe?

A barn's broad side, the damp

floor of a stable,

shit, mud and straw,

the boot's hard heel,

a heavy sky, fields

where thin rain falls

on great flat stones

turning them dark.

Could you repeat that?

A clapboard church

in evening light, bright

as the first hot star,

brown paper slapped

against barbed wire,

the stuttering clouds,

crows rising madly,

all at once, a consensus.

WE CAN'T TAKE OUR EYES OFF THEM

The thing about Indiana
        is there can be
no sunshine for two
        weeks straight.
But every morning
        the coffee shop signs
have been flipped:
        Yes! We're Open.
The eighteen wheelers
        throw up
misty sludge, and you have
        a choice:
the day is soft
        and gray or this
is going to be
        a long drive.
I watched my mother
        dip her comb
into a glass of beer
        for shine
before rolling her
        hair in curlers
with white whiskers.
        Twenty years later
she said, *It must be*
        something in the air
we breathe, upon
        learning of a fellow
cancer victim.
        The sign on the church
marquee: Get Rich
        By Counting Your
Blessings. It's a lot
        to absorb. Let's
not ignore spring
        when rivers

loosen their tongues.
        That's when we
fall to our knees. A crowd
        gathers around
the performers on Bourbon Street.
        Like stars, they
hold themselves still.
        The miracle
is not blinking. Later
        by the pool I was on
a mission:
        don't move
until the shade
        touches your toe. I admit
I wobbled
        as the courtyard
divided itself
        into dark and light.

FASTER

I don't know what we would call it, our philosophical
discussion prompted by a jar of single roses
sold in the checkout line at the drug store
next to the tabloids and mini flashlights,
which appeared to have some meaning,
a reference to something that wasn't quite clear.
Those deep red roses, each one in a clear plastic tube.
In the car you spoke of gardens, of dust and transgressions,
physicality, what's flawed, the bigger picture.
In the park I mentioned the steady thrumming
of insects, the continuous departures and arrivals,
and breath of all things. We took turns kicking the ball
back to the children when it rolled near our feet.
You pointed to the crack in the sidewalk, to a weed
poking through as if it were a big mistake
that needed to be corrected, a tragedy among
the many tragedies. We both leaned forward,
our ice cream melting faster than we could eat it.

On Not Being Coherent on Life or Death

Maybe there are two lives, I said,
each one clear and moving behind
the other like sliding glass doors.
Maybe in the great parking lot of life
we have conveniently ignored the sign:
For Visitors Only.
I may have made a mistake in talking
about the beauty in separation,
the terror of eternity
no matter what garden we're walking in.
It's hard to tell the make-believe
from the real, I added.
I tried examples: people without limbs,
dead deer at the side of the road, perfection
in the eagle's arc. Where are the riches
in this life? I asked, although it may have
sounded something like *screw the politicians*!
The sun was shining brilliantly through
the window and I wanted to lie down
and curl up like a cat and say
fuck it which I realized would be a mistake,
but I'd be throwing it out there
to loosen the bolt of anxiety.
I heard the shattering of glass, and in
another silence I heard a clock ticking.
Look, I said, finally,
we weren't wringing our hands
the infinite number of years
before we were born.
The water is fine, just fine, I assured.
The world does what it does, I concluded.
Nobody heard me mention the undulations
on the walls, the endless decoding.

NEIL DEGRASSE TYSON

It's some kind of psychedelic sunset, this shocking
           pink bath towel I hold in front of me
while the salesman is telling me

that everything on clearance is a final sale.
           And then I'm touching the hand towels
and washcloths, running my hand over

a rug's wavy nap, a rug that many people have
           rejected for their bathrooms. Why I'm folding
and refolding the towels trying for some kind

of supreme order among the chaos is a mystery.
           Oddly, I'm not thinking about the mistakes
I've made, mismatched décor being the least

egregious, but about astrophysics, more specifically
           about Neil deGrasse Tyson who explains
in plain English that less than a billionth of a second

after the big bang, all the matter and energy
           in the universe existed and then it slowly cooled
forming this solid blue-green earth. I'm thinking

about how long it took since that auspicious beginning
           for someone to invent the towel,
and then, fondly, about the towel-obsessed people

who got busy perfecting it, making it softer and more
           absorbent, so that what waits for me when I rise
up out of a steamy bath, water droplets sliding down

my arms and breasts and shoulders, is some comfort.
           What I reach for is something plush
that will hold me while my lungs contract and expand.

Equinox

I cheated on my life with another life.
In this new life, children shrieking in the pool
don't bother me. In fact, water itself is much less
frightening, more serene. I no longer care that the rain
is shameless in its excesses. I am bad at religion,
although I wasn't good at it in the old life either.
Except as a child when I knew what to do
with my hands at all times, when I knew how to
wear white despite the confusion about being a bride.
I marry the stars to infinity now with much more ease.
I'm sad all the time, but in a good way. In the old life
I was told to look at the sculptures, but I refused. Now
I see every winter tree, their tragic skeletal beauty,
and I hold that bright mass inside me. Always
my thoughts have been taut like kite string. When I close
my eyes, the corridors of light are primal. It's too much.
I used to ignore the phrase "a lifetime ago."
It's impossible to say where we are.

MARCH

That teenage couple under the bridge
is oh-so-oblivious to time.

His hand, her hands.
His mouth, her mouth.

In the future, the sweet smell of spring—
decay mixed with arrival—
will call up what can't be named.

The past will be a field each enters separately.

A raven's beak deep
into the warm blood of a rabbit,

not far from water rushing under a bridge.

Two

THE NEXT INFINITY

I.

All that talk about Jesus pointing to God
made us lighter. Or was it the horizon
stretching in every direction as we left church
and caravanned to the little country cemetery?

Or perhaps it was seeing the tractor's giant
wheels rolling over the fertile earth.
At first the rain fell like feathers
on the silver casket.

That was one infinity,

and we had to step over its broken glass.

II.

A violent storm of ash buried Pompeii.
We walk over the rubble
and pause to admire the frescoes
adorning the doors in the brothel.
Doors
lead to other doors,
where stark light
cuts in jagged halves.

We shield our eyes but hold that infinity close.

III.

Rise from the anesthesia
into a buzzing fog. No clarity
just babbling
and involuntary tears.
Whimper *It's cold, so cold.*

Doctor, how often do we change the gauze?

The water beneath that infinity is cold and you'll come up begging.

IV.

For anyone who's ever felt starved,
or brittle, or dreaded a day without parabola,
embrace infinity's echo, like shallow
breath, or darkness in the pit of forever.

V.

Stick a bookmark in this infinity

and come back to it after

the dark red claw of passion leaves its mark.

Beautiful terror of a radiant half moon.
Beautiful emptiness of a silent piano.

Beautiful telescoping of a tongue
where innumerable stars wink
along the untamed ocean of flesh.

Impossible to avoid all the broken glass
hidden in the sand, but carry on dancing.

Carry on fumbling in the dark

as if no candles could be had,

for who can resist a violet night?

Who can resist singing just one note
when the lightning
is so white, so gold,
so white-gold?

VI.

An autopsy of infinity would uncover a bare, stripped down field.

VII.

What defines your next to nothing?

The prayer, the hymn, or the ashes in the box?

Maybe the wind that streams over the tilled field.

Just a little anesthesia, please.
Undress the story, and place an *
over each unstressed syllable.

The next infinity will burn out like a super nova.
Its buzz will be low and distant like a spectral heart.

Beneath the quiet, earth.

Beneath the shut eyes,
a kind of darkness
that sparks
another darkness,
and that darkness
is infinite.

AM

You may remember the scratchy sound of AM radio.
You'd catch a scrap of song as you passed
a car window. Often, there would be a woman
or man inside, smoking. They punched
the car lighter, waited, and then touched the tip
of their cigarette to a glowing circle of orange.
They stared ahead as the smoke
slipped from between their lips.
That's gone now, right?
Not radios and cigarettes, but the past,
small and dim. The song,
in its purity, impossible to locate.

Always in Motion

You will be lost
in the wild vibrations
particularly in spring
when everything dirty
like an old penny
is suddenly lush
and green,

and when, more than ever,
you live your life
by light and dark.
The sun rounds
the tall maple, a cardinal
sings sweetly, rhythmically,
throat full of bubbles,

and you ask it why it has to be
so driven, so compulsive,
but you're just projecting, aren't you?
It's a breeze
we say when things are easy,
lighter than we thought,
and after the rain

has ended, after
the doors and windows
have been opened, our bodies
make long shadows
on the driveway,
and a secret
in the palm,

or on the breath
is light as a dime
and easily lost. The body
is a vessel. The body
is the boat, or the impossible
glass bottle that surrounds the boat,

one world inside another.
Down below,
let the burning lamp
throw yellow light
at the black windows, let
blue ink stain the page.

Let the rain
turn the hard sea
the color of nickel . . .
Nature is innocent
and culpable
when wind and rain lash
the weakest limbs.

Some things you can't keep down.
You hear the crumpled
cellophane
in the next room
expanding,
making room
for itself.

Just the Facts

In the chain of time a woman is born in 1886
on the west coast, and her great-grandson

is shot out east in a Jersey parking lot.
And in between those two events, many people

have rocked back and forth, heel to toe, jingling
the change in their pockets, waiting for the bride

to appear at the end of the aisle. You have been
to the fair, haven't you? Taken your turn on a big,

bright wheel that floats you to the edge of forever,
your home town diminishing as you rise.

Your body throws down a shadow dimmed
by an artificial incandescent glow.

You can't stop the whirring, the endless circles.
That's the difficulty of this Earth.

IN DECEMBER, IT'S EASY TO DROWN

In December, on a long stretch of highway,
I drown in dark.
Up ahead a police car lights up

its disturbing strobe
redblueredblueredblue.

The red one rings its thunderous bell
while the blue goes begging
for a beautiful soul,
or is it the other way around?

I arrive early and sit in my car
looking at the sky.

My brain is even less inviting
when it's wild with dark birds flitting
through its spangled hallways.

I eventually enter the house
with a bottle of wine
and spill it over white linen.

I can't say now what I was thinking.

BLACK FLOWERING

When she enters that strange country,
the people line up red-faced, scraping
mud off the heels of their boots.

      The past gets uprooted like a tree and then pushed under like a stone.

She enters the world on a fine blue current.
Crusted, fists clenched,
her slick, wet body stains
the cold slab of the table,
the white towels.
Blindness results from the jolt of birth.

      Everyone is so serious, so intense.

They give her a membership card
in the form of a thin white band at the ankle.
Her name, okay, but also *I've crossed over.*

When the door opens, the air is electric.
She sees the gold. She sees a man
in a wheelchair, a man
with a steel hook for a hand.
She can't shake the images.
She feels the rush like a knife of wind
slicing the yellow grasses.

      She flings open her arms because she wants to fly.

      She thinks she can flee.

Heat. Cheeks flushed.
With his body he pins her hard
to the bed,
the floor,
the wall.
Keep your eyes open.
Flickering candles throw shadows around the room.

Who will dip her hand in that light?
Who will bring her hand to her mouth so she can taste it?

Before she could speak, sunlight fell through
the towering trees. She had to look up into the black flowering,
stare through the pocked and evaporating leaves.

Her breath fans out over the surface of a mirror.

She learns proficiency.
She places herself between the wound and whatever caused it.

She understands she will never climb out of that beauty. . .

A mother bears down, the head crowns.
A baby slips into the open air. She'll want to be touched
way back at the end of her mind.
She'll want to be ground down
and then polished like a stone.

What would it take to be cured?

What if she were healed?

Blood and White Paper

Isn't predictability great?

Of course there's a wedding
and glasses of champagne,
bubbles rising like some surreal
snowfall, and on the other side

of the world, there's half a moon
in a sapphire sky over
a withering red barn.

Of course there's a hungry baby
suckling, its fontanel fusing, its little
heart an inflating balloon.

Right here, right now
in the middle of the day in my
neighborhood supermarket
I say "that one" to the butcher
and he starts his ritual

of blood and white paper,
the shopping cart clack-clacking
past stacked soda cartons.

A celebratory toast, bright
celestial glow, the division of cells,

a knife.

MOURNING NEVER SKIPS A GENERATION

Christmas tree needles
on the floor in July.

Green weeds sprouting through the split
asphalt at the 7-11.

Flecks of dust in a bar of sunlight.

The glue traps, too.
Unlucky mice.

My mother's string of pearls.
My mother's Chanel No. 5.

My mother the floating hostess,
martinis flowing
into all the diseased organs.

She carried her cigarettes from room
to room like a rabbit's foot.

I remember the dry cough, the dirty
patches of snow outside the window.

And Lead Us Not

As backdrop,
what was called a locomotive then, black
and burning through a field.

A dusty photo shoot, light bright as milk.
A woman by the door in a black coat
and white dress among the rocks and weeds

in a blur of heat with a beauty hard to believe,
therefore difficult. "Tell me the truth," my father urged,
convincing me I could not be trusted.

I looked beyond him over his shoulder
where the angels were beating their wings
to a silent choir. They told me if I wore

the scapular at death, the Virgin
Mary would wave me into heaven, no barriers.
I couldn't figure out how to be more innocent.

I draped a towel around my head to look like a nun.
I tied a cloth around my eyes so I couldn't see. I washed in cold
water, ordered plain milk instead of chocolate.

I folded my body over a wooden table—
pelvis, chin, tongue . . . I would be like something dying, its mouth
parted, calling the blue plum of June. They cut off

my hair every summer,
just as it was starting to swing. *You're such a pixie.* Prepare
for nighttime, prepare for the moon,

its white light on my pillow like a dream,
beautiful and therefore difficult.
I take chalk, some black ink, black like a train,

black like smoke and broken bark,
and in the slanted dark draw a face, my face in the mirror,
face in my father's hands.

Paris Fugue

I digest the warm, broken pieces of the sky.

      Light keeps falling through my fingers.

A woman on the subway can't believe her son's beautiful face.

      Let the roses do the talking, let the peonies.

The sheets on the bed are tucked. The housekeeper keeps closing the window.

      Something light as breath survives underneath all the stone.

She lifts his chin, brushes his bangs with her fingers.

      The hotel room is small, bereft of flowers.

Something final keeps falling from the portrait, from the voices.

      The carrousel is still, but the legs and faces of the horses are in motion.

His face, as if she were unwrapping something fragile from its tissue paper.

      People stand on the bridges and wave to the boats.

Hundreds of roses stacked, piles of roses. Merci bien.

      There is no end to the life of a fountain; it keeps spewing, gurgling.

She has a book in her lap and urges him to read.

      The window faces west. In the evening, a baby cries and cries.

Maps keep falling from my hands, my pockets.

      The portrait goes on even after you turn away and descend the stairs.

He reads a couple of words and then gives up. His voice is like calm water.

There are pearls in the shop windows, masks, and angels' wings.

I see the dark side of light in the church windows. Jesus raises a finger.

The cat's mewing is like light rain in the courtyard.

She reads to him. He twirls a strand of her hair with his finger.

The wind is feeling, brushing all the stone.

It's gone, it's over the bridge, it's out of the frame.

How can it fail, the fountain's pouty lip?

He lays his head down on top of the book.

I'm putting my faith in the broken wheel, the stacked silk and lace.

Comes the light and the wings and the stone horses.

He is falling into a dream he will never remember.

Comes the crow fuming in the cemetery tree.

Holy Week

It's no mystery
the snow in April
        coating the trees—winnowing
the weaker limbs—exquisitely,

        reminds me of the Bishop
from Rome
        who told the movie audience
that Scorsese's *The Last Temptation of Christ*
        was too violent.

Not for Jesus Christ, he kept repeating.

        But didn't the nuns emphasize
the crown of thorns, the spitting,
        the thirty-nine lashes, the nails,

the bleeding, the collapse?

Here's how I remember that art:

        Mary crumpled.

Her son limp, his head in her hands,
        the cracked sky raining—

                        then a silence
in which even the angels falter.

        That privacy, that solitude
sends her back in time,
        and then forward

        to the lilies,
                astonishingly loud,
to the white

        and widening light.

THE SPACES BETWEEN

the maple seeds spiral

down furiously

determined to take hold

    a few fall through

the basketball net

    onto the concrete

which reminds me

of the woman at the curb

sitting in her car

    with her palm out

separating the white pills

    from the orange

with her index finger

which reminds me

of sunny days when

    I try to see behind

sunglasses but all I get

    is reflection   clouds

birds making their way.

Early Evening, April

Make no mistake—the hostas
start as nubs, brass knuckles
punching through the spring

soil, but they soon learn to open
their soft green hands.

In their hard teenage years, they'll sprout
a single spike and put everything they've got
into their short

purple bloom-life before growing
large, complacent.

Oh, I think ahead now from the glider chair:
the stalks will turn brittle and snap.

It's easy to see them splayed and yellow.
It's safe to assume the ground will be cold.

WE HAVE HOPE ON HOLD

Hope, as it turns out, is a person.

I'm in my car listening to the bubbly disc-jockey
who is talking with Hope, telling her she has won
a semi-fabulous prize,

and I've lost faith in the bargain
between drivers
the one that says you and I
will stop
will signal
will move at a reasonable rate.
I comply, I really do,

despite the fact that I've become skittish
on two-way streets
and roundabouts
trying not to get distracted
by clever billboards
such as "Be a Fountain, Not a Drain."

I can't remember ever being as ebullient
as a fountain, spilling enthusiastically
all over creation, although I'm proud to say
that I've never really dragged anyone down
or sent anyone into a spiral,
unless you count the heart-to-heart
I had with Pamela when I said,
really now, listen, I'm serious, the Botox injections
have to stop
which clogged both of us up with
shame and self-doubt.

Sometimes I think today I'll win a small
cash prize on a scratch-off lottery ticket. Or, this is the day
I get T-boned at a four-way stop.

I'm not negative, really. I can hold out for a thing with feathers

because Hope is saying *wonderful, wonderful,*
        thank you so much.

THREE

THIRD WAVE

Yet, I like
those photos
in fashion magazines
where scenes are artsy
and unreal.
No context.
Models in mid-air,
five-inch heels,
eyes outlined in
bright orange.
Or the ashen-faced,
androgynous ones
with no breasts,
no make-up,
hair sleeked back,
who appear to have curvature
of the spine.
They're all reduction
standing there
in pale underwear, their
fingers on each other's
faces. Or hippie waifs
with kinky hair posing
on rural porches wearing
bold prints. Ladies
with red lips lounging
on tabletops, floating
in pools or flooded
rooms appearing
not sad, but blank.
They're not of this world,
are they? They're not
of this mid-western
summer, this land
of a thousand insects
and grieving tomatoes.

                    They're not bothered
by fierce flies
                    and frightened cats.
They're not fascinated
                    by the disc-shaped
vacuum wandering the linoleum
                    for hours until
it stalls in the corner
                    with the dust
and the dim light.

INSTRUCTIONS

I don't know why I think of her now, in mid-May, while
I sit in the yard drinking a cold beer, but she comes to mind,
S, who rolled a joint and offered it to me in the bedroom
that she locked with a key tied to a string worn around
her neck to keep her mother out and her sister, her fraternal
twin, another S, who was taller, thinner, more hip, who
walked around with her eyes half-closed on purpose, who
flunked most everything but wanted to learn French, who
wore floppy hats and silver bracelets and purple bell-bottoms.
But S didn't have any papers, so she pulled the cover off
a tampon and fumbled for awhile, and I sat on the rug
watching until she had something that resembled a cigarette,
and I tried to inhale the way she instructed, but I coughed
and she did too, and we laughed, and she opened the window
wider because her mother was yelling from the bottom
of the stairs, and she yelled back that she was burning incense,
and I think of her because of this heat wave, or the pungent
lilacs, or maybe the dandelions' fragile, ghostly heads.

LOCATION

In the car, the faceless woman—the voice of GPS—
  is apologizing for not being able to understand me.

(*I'm sorry. Is that right? Say* yes *or* no.)

I admit to having trouble getting my own location.

I'm forever purchasing the same one-way ticket
  to the land of Sacrifice All For Art.

I understand. I'm misunderstood.

I'm like a dog on a choke collar.
  I'm overwrought. I'm anxious to get *anywhere*.

The little boy at the fair is begging to go on a rocket ride.

That kind of travel produces an adrenaline surge.

When I enter the time machine, I mix up a darker palette.

My mother in the courtyard, naked,
  one hand hiding her missing breast.

Here I go cleaving my way through the wilderness.

DIVINE

They are not capable of leading a double life.
These two love-sick teenagers standing
in the shadows, away from the sun,
away from the river that receives brown
sludge from its tributaries. They can't be anywhere but here,
and she can't love anyone other than this boy
who has perfected a cool way of jerking his head
to get the hair out of his eyes.
He grabs her open coat by the collar
and pulls her close. Several silver hooks cling
the edge of her ear. They both bring cigarettes
to their mouths and can't imagine a day when
they will tire of the other's complex moods,
untangling them like a knot, a knot
on a thin gold chain,
a knot they have to bring
into better light, and then find
a needle to insert
into the heart of it.

Yellow

The dress was either yellow
like a canary or like the cat
that ate the canary.
What I remember him saying
was *You look like an Easter egg,*
in a not-so-flattering tone.
That coming from a factory rat,
a third-shifter, who referred to the job
as the gift that keeps on giving
after he coughed up phlegm
into a white handkerchief.
Do you like butter? a friend asked
me as she held a dandelion
underneath my chin looking
for a sign. When she got bored
she pulled up tulips and daisies
from the neighbors' yards and gave them
to her mother who half-scolded her
because she knew the pleasures
of coveting objects mostly dreamt
about while she sat at the kitchen table
twisting her straw-colored hair
with an index finger and drinking pale beer.
The house always smelled of lemons.
That's the truth, she liked to say,
while clutching a big box of matches
out on the back stoop. Truth, however,
made irregular and brief appearances,
speeding through as a car might
trying to outrun the red.
But, really, there's nothing false
about striking a match, letting
it fall, watching the flame flare
and then die out. Who wouldn't
go through a box just for fun?
I know, I know, plenty.
Cowards.

POSTERITY

Where I come from everything is an emergency that can't be reined.

A mile away is a church with long lines at the confessionals,
a parking lot with only so many ways out.

The children poke sticks at endless carcasses
and are told not to touch them.

Springtime throws out its excess like a kind of applause.

The fathers, muscular and glowing, gather at dusk
to make sure they are hating the same world.

We all have bodies, so someone gets the camera:
the family in front of the new car.

Someone has to pack all of it into that tiny frame.

LIGHT

A black-winged grief clings
to a stripped-down tree.

The violet sky, the cobalt sea
are messages from beauty.

My father's history,
my father's younger heart—

feelings he couldn't name,
or named too clearly.

Martinis. Another *martoony*.

When he was drunk he said, Oh, your mother's alright,
but I don't like niggers, don't like those people.

A geography of the heart.
A geography of flight.

Thunderclouds over a cornfield,
but the sun leaks through.

Melancholy as a form of happiness.

I'm an addict.

An addict of what?

*I don't know, but as I descend into the light
I can step out of this body.*

A Narrative for the New Century

I can't help but stare
at the crucifix above
the exit sign.

But it doesn't tell the whole truth.

Neither does the blown-out tire
at the side of the road,

or the clump of gray feathers in the grass,

or the marigolds shaking in the wind.

If I could spend hours
looking at the starlings
shape-shift
in the blue dusk, I would end up
rooting for the mystery of flight.

  ∾

Instead I walk the museum with my hands
clasped behind my back
saying nothing, talking to no one,
nodding politely to strangers, bending
in close to a streak of yellow
whispering to myself, "oh, that's interesting,"
so that I don't get lost.

The docent walks the long corridor,
The doorman checks his watch,
The security guard adjusts his earplug

and

young men wave guns over the asphalt.
They tease an alphabet out of the dark,
become fluent in violence.

And so

the static begins, the constant refrain.
Violence has become *story*,
a narrative for the new century.

∽

If I could just see the inside of my head.

If I could harvest the mind's flutter,
the luminous, winged thoughts that, I swear,
I can feel in my breastbone.

I would read the map
of the old century, its pages turned yellow,
its roads no longer relevant,

and I'm starting to wonder if I'm in this poem
all by myself.

But don't we, all of us,
want to tunnel out of this desert,
this neatly folded place,

armed with a box of charcoals
to shade in a sound, the low-throated jabbering
of pigeons swarming
at our feet, bobbing their beautiful heads?

I know that it's too dramatic to say
that my thoughts scatter
like a fistful of jacks
thrown across a linoleum floor.

It's my own fault.
I forgot to breathe.
I forgot to change
the channel, ignore
the graffiti,
take a different route.

~

The hypnotist's watch
keeps us tuned to what is immaculate

despite the blood that
pools on the asphalt
without anyone's permission,

that luster.

In the hushed room of the museum,
I look at Cezanne's spilled apples and peaches.
The yellow is born out of the sun.
The red is born out of the stars.
He'd like to welcome me to his table,
to his soft light.

I don't leave without genuflecting.
I don't leave without seeking out
his cupid with no arms.

The eye chooses . . .

~

Every day we enter the courtroom

and witness the endless grieving, a mother's grief,
grief that pulls at her mouth, grief
that builds a city inside her,
a city for a new century.

There's static, there's breaking news, there's live feed.

There are survivors who are on the brink
of living half-lives.

They are left to construct an alphabet
that makes sense of blood
and absence.

Turn it
around
and around,
a stone in the hand . . .

The bodies keep falling,
crumpling. The fine dust of chance
settles and it makes no noise,

and we want to be whole, we want to live.

≈

I want to live

to climb the steep museum steps, sit
at the long Thanksgiving table, flex
my dirt-caked hands.

I want to ride the train that comes slowly to a halt,
its lights flicker

and then silence.

Like a curtain rising on the greatest of dramas,
the cars light up again,
and go streaming into the dark.

And if the postcard never gets written
And if what ends here does not continue
And if we could delay the past from arriving

~

Nothing criminal in trying to crack
the world's schematics,
but the tumblers were never
meant to be heard.

No point in finding the longevity line
in a palm.

And if the body becomes its own wonder
And if the lone gunman has nothing to say
And if the master has no one who listens

we'll roll out the dissecting table one more time.

I ask, even in the half-light, if we are keepers of our own asylum.
Inside the new century, the orchestra never

lets up, so we dance. Or whatever it is we can do now.

The Sky Is Where I Left It

I see the reflection of birds
in my computer screen,

and they move like floaters.

The nurse says, "Do you ever experience floaters?"

I once pinched a dot of sunlight on the carpet
thinking it was a dime.

In every face there is a shared inheritance.
The claw is barely visible.

I say this life is hard, but we can't set up a trading post for grief.

As fire ravages the west,

ash drifts upward

tempting the eye to follow what's strange, illusory.

OFTEN ENOUGH

You enter the dingy train station
       With its high wooden benches,

Shaking your wristwatch, holding it to your ear.
       That was long ago, when you traveled the country

Of ruins, folding and unfolding your lover's letter
       While something fluttered over the dry lawn.

That kind of afternoon will stamp your ticket
       More than any shock of beauty.

Better to decompose right there, sunlight
       Punching through the dirty glass.

A long, hot breeze passes through the needle of summer.
       It blooms in brilliant disguise

As you lie down in the drawer of night, a perfect unlit candle,
       Away from the flesh of any church.

Soon morning opens up, crusted bone
       Of the desert, white as death . . .

STAR

When the world is too big,
      go about your business.

Grip the handle of a rake or a broom.

When the world is too small,
      let a stone fall
from your hand, or set
      a ball in motion.

Release a creature from its cage.

When you find yourself calm,
      and when you can breathe, stretch

out under a tree and be
      that crystalline white star

forming on a windshield,

born out of accident,

      creeping away from the center.

FOUR

CLOSE CALL

We had never been
nor would we ever be
that close to each other again.
She ran the stop sign,
and we both slammed on the brakes
before staring at each other's
changed face.

Once, while tying her shoes, a friend
said that God had been watching out
for her. That morning roads had been slick,
and her car slid into the guard rail,
but she walked away unhurt. ·

I just make it up as I go, say the careless.
Ice makes it up as it goes along.

Turn the corner, ice.

Some days you're forced to memorize
a face struck dumb.`

Some days the news is terrible.

Some days you don't even know you're alive.

'YOUR CHARM HAD NOT GONE UNNOTICED BY THE ANGEL'
(fortune cookie)

The angel?
When I told the apologetic sales clerk
not to worry,
that I had grown accustomed
to poor service,
when I screamed *fuck you*
at the automated voice
that wanted me to choose
from the following menu, when
I lapsed into total silence for days
because the estimate came in too high,
when I declared unequivocally
that I would never vote again,
no one was noticing my charm,
least of all an angel.
The angel.

Clearly, I'm in need of help.

I need a cop to chalk a circle
around my dead compassion.
A cold thumb and forefinger to snuff
the hot wick of my anger. A pool shark
to teach me the geometry of aim.
I need the angel to climb down
from the ethereal clouds, the ones
I used to see on holy cards,
so we can visit.
I'll pour the whiskey.
I'll fluff up the sofa pillows.

I've never touched a wing.

Airport Selfie

You, but dark—
your own shadow on the carpet.

A photo of you taking a photo.

Check your own bag, please.
Check one: You are
a) self-contained b) self-motivated
c) self-willed d) self-seeking
e) all of the above.

You come and go *with* incident.
You hold your phone-camera at arm's length.
There you are buying a magazine.
You boarding.
You holding up a drink.
I got the window seat!

That's the cosmos above you.

That's the plane's shadow moving across patches
of farmland, mile by mile,
stealing space.

That's a prayer on your tongue.

That little not-yet is you traversing cyberspace.

BLINK

Somewhere someone is fretting
      over the pastel towels

in the guest bathroom.
      Frost and dust
settle on window panes in patterns.

"So, this is death," she might have thought
      seconds before the EMTs arrived.

She tries hard to remember the exact words . . .
      Nobody is one thing all the time.

      Ocean waves fold over
making sounds that are hypnotic. Fresh lemonade
      served over crushed ice. Dark, dried-up

fruit litters the rural landscape.
      Gather them up
and countless others appear.

      Do not use the bathroom.
      Do not touch the fingertip towels.

She gulps air and gains a bird's eye view.

What would keep the churches beautiful and silent?

The Knife Came Out Clean

I'm an accident in somebody else's Sunday afternoon.

When the snow melts, it's a relief, but the world
reveals its sadder colors—pale yellow and gray.

Someone appears in a red coat to provide contrast,
changing the landscape.

But, I digress. I'm never sure how the mind works.

That accident? I'm looking at old pictures
I've seen a hundred times. There's our baby

and the tall stranger in blue behind her.
He's a fixture forever in our archives.

To the left of the merry-go-round,
and on the crooked street, I'm a minor character,

off center—away from the real subject.

A woman in the playground is cutting a cake.
There's a birthday party underway,

the tulips' heads are bowed, and I walk the incline.
I'm on my way out of the frame.

DRAIN

The sink is gurgling, whispering
the names of the dead,

so I set the book down and flip
the light switch over this cathedral
where sin is born and forgiven.

Pieces of bread, swollen, float
among seeds and peppers
and pork fat—regurgitation.

My mind turns to things that began
in water and have come up
bigger, hungrier, without shame.

Missing

A little moonlight through the trees, maybe.

Scattered tufts of grass in an open field.

What pecks, bores, or burrows
raised its head to footsteps, to a rustling.

Real   body found   missing

her body   remote area

Real disappearance

inside   pushed Real down

Real dead   Real body   rode

cause   Real   declined bed

Real changed

When the hard earth began to soften,
there was endless talk about the weather.

The skin of white over the field meant no harm.

PERFECT DARK MORNING

The world waits always,
and always,
with some hesitation,
we meet the world.

Quietly, alone,
the worker finishes his cigarette,
stubs it out
and pushes away from the truck

to begin mowing lawns
still wet
and shaking with dew.

THE MULTITUDES

Come into the light we say
when we want to get a better look.

That way it will become clear.

A birthday cake purposely tossed
into the snow
makes a clear statement

as do the red high heels and those plastic tiaras
that invite make believe. But, really,
who doesn't want to be someone else?

My mother dragging on a cigarette for thirty-four years.

You read the entire history of being
on a dead gray face.

Everything in moderation.

The sun is *disinterested.* The whole
stupid planet could disappear.

Hello! we say when we're in the presence of the obvious.

Over there, the multitudes, the specks
of dust we'd like to separate ourselves from.

Cut crystal takes its turn with light.
It's how we postpone sweeping up the ashes.

EARTHLY

You notice a wine stain on the kitchen countertop, a round
purple ring like night itself. There's a temptation to make more rings
and darker nights. You take stock in the minor key because the moon
does, pulling up its long white glove and settling into a box seat
for the endless intergalactic arias. You love wan faces and pale
hands that flare under the footlights. You hold still as you wait
for the slim finger of lake to flash nickel gray, and for the silver
rowboat's bright sheen. That kind of muscle keeps you from
collapsing under the weight of a star. Look at the map: You are here.

Roll Away the Stone

The next time someone tells you you're a nobody from nowhere,
tell them you saw J-E-S-U-S in giant red letters across a white
trailer truck. If you're a sucker for symbolism, that's a *heavy load*,
man. Pure rapture. It's true, corn can be boring, but when the fog
lifts, the sheer repetition of the overstocked fields suggests,
beautifully, form and function. Birds swoop down to the dusty
dirt demanding to see the wine list. The scarecrow, too, wants a seat
at the table, but not before showing you his wound, lifting one corner
of his tattered blue shirt as if to say he's all in, body and soul.

Dear Diary,

There's a diorama nestled in my heart.
See the white barn, the broken wheel
and the furrowed field? The figure
leaning against the fence points
to her water heart full of tiny bubbles.
The striped fish dart around a little
blue-green treasure chest where inside,
standing on plush velvet, a magician
wearing white gloves looks up
at the night sky and pulls coins
from behind the ears of endless stars.

Acknowledgments

Many thanks to the editors of the following publications in which these poems, sometimes in different versions, first appeared:

5 AM / "Faster"
American Literary Review / "Often Enough"
California Quarterly /"Airport Selfie"; "Close Call"
Chariton Review / "On Not Being Coherent on Life or Death"
Cimarron Review / "Love is Blue"; "Instructions"; "Divine"
Columbia Poetry Review / "We're Okay in the Heartland"
december / "Roll Away the Stone"
The Del Sol Review / "Yellow"
Eclipse / "Skin"; "The Next Infinity"
*Fifth Wednesday Journa*l/ "Posterity"
The Laurel Review / "Poll"
The MacGuffin / 'Your charm had not gone unnoticed by the angel'
Midwestern Gothic / "March"
Permafrost / "Just the Facts"
Poetry East / "Right Angels"; "Blink"; "Perfect Dark Morning"; "Holy Week"; "Drain"
POOL / "The Multitudes"; "We Can't Take Our Eyes Off Them"
Salamander / "Paris Fugue"
South Dakota Review / "Same Rain, Same City"
The Wabash Watershed / "The Sky is Where I Left It"; "Location"; (Special Poetry Feature with Poet Laureate of Indiana, George Kalamaras); "Missing" (Second Place Winner in the Social Justice category, 2015 Indiana Poetry Awards)

About the Author

Born in Detroit, Nancy Botkin earned a BA in English from Michigan State University and a Master of Liberal Studies from Indiana University South Bend. Her first full-length poetry collection, *Parts That Were Once Whole* (2007), included "Poem With Light and Dark," which won the Maize First Place Poetry Prize sponsored by the Writers' Center of Indiana. Her poetry has been published in former U.S. Poet Laureate Ted Kooser's column, "American Life in Poetry."

Botkin's work has been published in various journals such as *Poetry*, *Poetry East*, the *Laurel Review*, and the *American Literary Review*. She is currently a senior lecturer in the English department at Indiana University South Bend, where she has been teaching since 1991. She will soon retire from teaching to devote more time to poetry, art, travel, and her grandson.